Facts About the Stingray

By Lisa Strattin

© 2019 Lisa Strattin

FREE BOOK

FREE FOR ALL SUBSCRIBERS

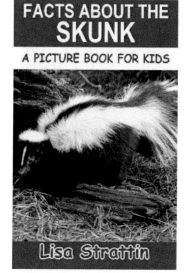

LisaStrattin.com/Subscribe-Here

BOX SET

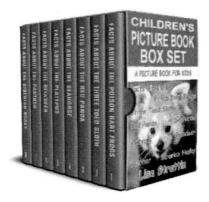

- FACTS ABOUT THE POISON DART FROGS
- FACTS ABOUT THE THREE TOED SLOTH
- FACTS ABOUT THE RED PANDA
- FACTS ABOUT THE SEAHORSE
- FACTS ABOUT THE PLATYPUS
- FACTS ABOUT THE REINDEER
- FACTS ABOUT THE PANTHER
- FACTS ABOUT THE SIBERIAN HUSKY

LisaStrattin.com/BookBundle

Facts for Kids Picture Books by Lisa Strattin

Little Blue Penguin, Vol 92

Chipmunk, Vol 5

Frilled Lizard, Vol 39

Blue and Gold Macaw, Vol 13

Poison Dart Frogs, Vol 50

Blue Tarantula, Vol 115

African Elephants, Vol 8

Amur Leopard, Vol 89

Sabre Tooth Tiger, Vol 167

Baboon, Vol 174

Sign Up for New Release Emails Here

LisaStrattin.com/subscribe-here

IMAGEs ADDITIONAL PUBLIC DOMAIN

Contents

INTRODUCTION

The stingray is a very flat fish found in warmer waters around the world. The stingray belongs to the same group of fish as other ray and are believed to be closely related to sharks.

CHARACTERISTICS

The stingray is most well-known for the stinger on the end of their tail. They use the stinger to pierce through and stop prey before it can escape. So, it is the way for the stingray to get food as well as to protect itself.

APPEARANCE

The stingray's stinger is razor-sharp, barbed or serrated and attached to the stingray's long, thin tail. This means the animal can whip it's stinger to pretty much anywhere, quickly as the tail of the stingray is extremely agile and very flexible!

The size of a sting really depends on the species of stingray. Some species in the deep ocean get up to 14 feet long, including the tail, and these naturally have a larger stinger. The smaller species tend to have small stingers, so the stinger is truly relevant to the size of the body of the particular stingray.

14

BREEDING

Stingrays breed during the winter months and the female gives birth to live babies, usually between 5 and 15 baby stingrays. This is called a litter. The baby stingrays develop inside the mother for around 9 months. The babies are fed milk inside the womb of the female stingray. When the babies are born, they are able to swim about and begin hunting with their mother immediately.

16

LIFE SPAN

Stingrays live for 15 to 25 years. This can depend on the species and the environment where a specific stingray lives.

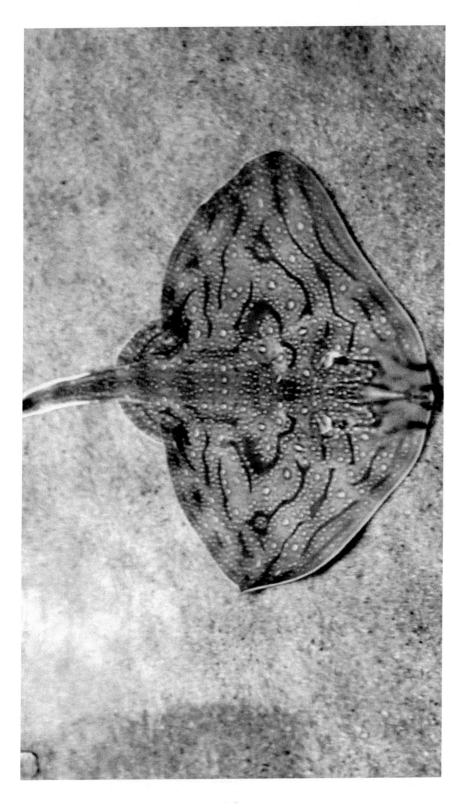

SIZE

Stingrays can be 20 inches long to over 6 feet and weigh between 55 pounds to over 200 pounds. They don't really look like they weigh that much in the pictures, do they?

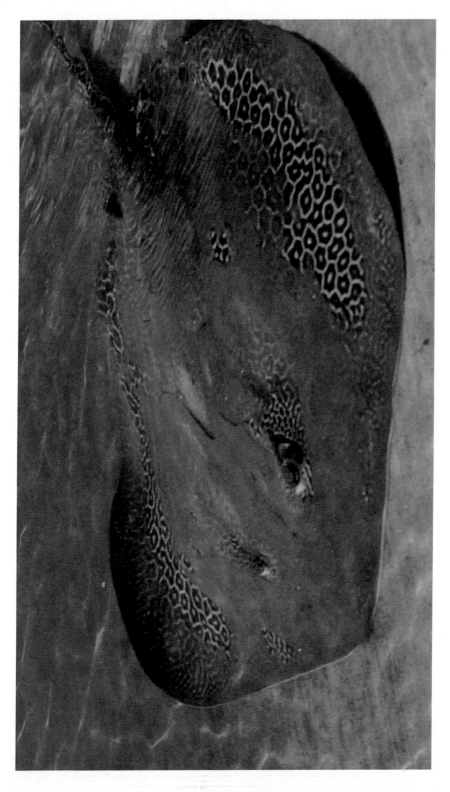

HABITAT

The stingray lives in the warm tropical waters around the world, generally in the deeper waters rather than the shallows. When the weather begins to cool in the winter season, the stingray retreats further into the depths of the ocean, searching for warmer waters.

DIET

The stingray is carnivorous. This means that they eat other animals and not plants. They prey on a wide variety of species in the sea including crabs, mollusks, clams, oysters, snails and some species of fish.

ENEMIES

The stingray does not have many natural predators in its native environment, mainly due to its large size. They are also able to use their flat body shape to their advantage; by resting on the sea floor, they are able to hide from predators while watching for potential prey.

The main predators of the stingrays are sharks, seals, sea lions and large species of carnivorous fish. These animals are about mostly larger than the stingray so can take control in a confrontation.

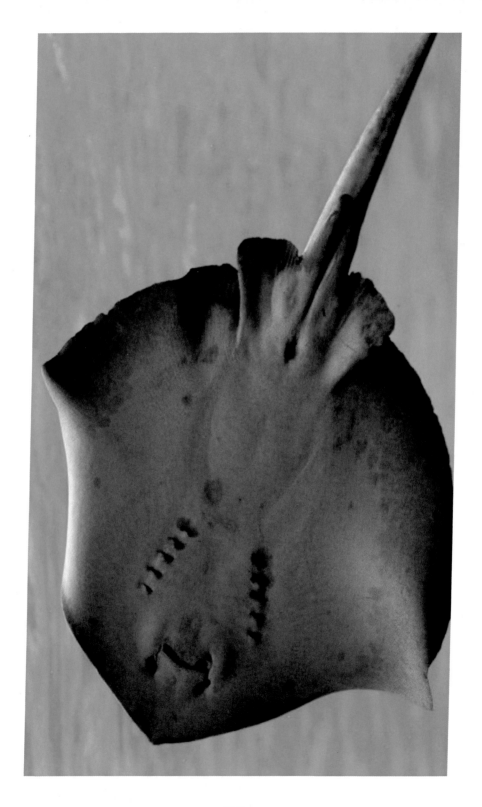

SUITABILITY AS PETS

Nope, not a good choice for a pet. You can see them at many zoos and aquariums if you want to watch them up close. In some aquariums and habitats, you are even allowed to reach into the water and pet them as they swim by!

28

COLOR ME

COLOR ME

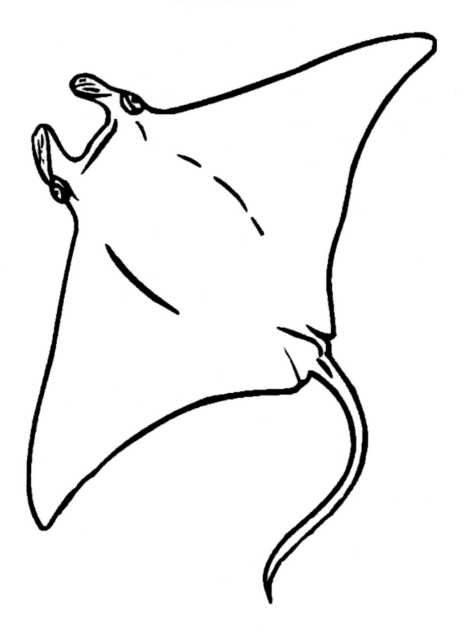

COLOR ME

COLOR ME

COLOR ME

COLOR ME

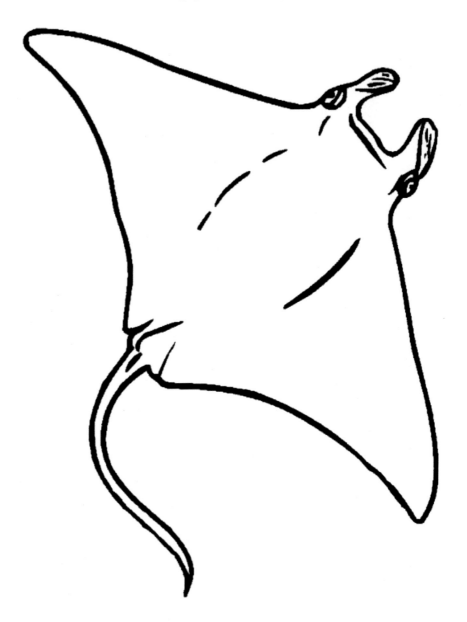

COLOR ME

COLOR ME

COLOR ME

COLOR ME

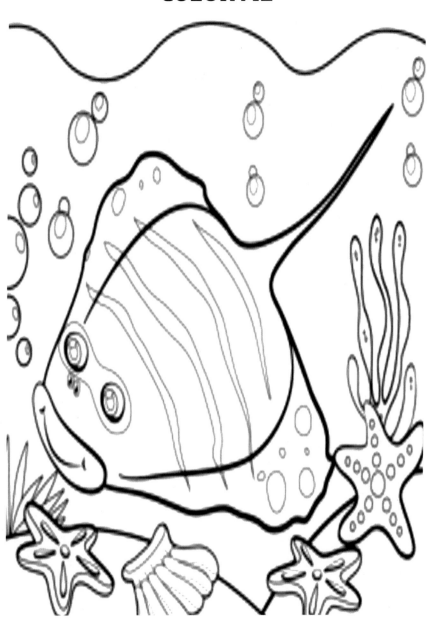

Please leave me a review here:

LisaStrattin.com/Review-Vol-250

For more Kindle Downloads Visit Lisa Strattin Author Page on Amazon Author Central

amazon.com/author/lisastrattin

To see upcoming titles, visit my website at LisaStrattin.com– most books available on Kindle!

LisaStrattin.com

FREE BOOK

FOR ALL SUBSCRIBERS – SIGN UP NOW

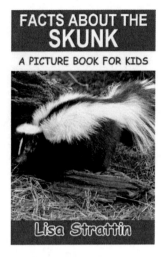

LisaStrattin.com/Subscribe-Here

LisaStrattin.com/Facebook

LisaStrattin.com/Youtube

Made in the USA
Monee, IL
17 May 2022

96608951R00026